iMath Readers

The Garden Club:
Operations with Fractions

by Renata Brunner-Jass

Content Consultant
David T. Hughes

Norwood House Press
PO Box 316598
Chicago, IL 60631

For information regarding Norwood House Press, please visit our website at
www.norwoodhousepress.com or call 866-565-2900.

Special thanks to: Heidi Doyle
Production Management: Six Red Marbles
Editors: Linda Bullock and Kendra Muntz
Printed in Heshan City, Guangdong, China. 208N—012013

Library of Congress Cataloging–in-Publication Data

Brunner-Jass, Renata.

  The garden club: operations with fractions/by Renata Brunner-Jass; content
  consultant, David Hughes, mathematics curriculum specialist.
  pages cm.—(iMath)

  Audience: 10–12
  Audience: Grade 4 to 6

  Summary: "The mathematical concept of equivalent fractions is introduced
  as students describe how they use both mixed and improper fractions to
  plant a vegetable garden at their school. Readers also learn the least common
  multiple, greatest common multiple, and ratios. This book includes a discover
  activity, a science connection, and mathematical vocabulary introduction"—
  Provided by publisher.

  Includes bibliographical references and index.

  ISBN 978-1-59953-570-8 (library edition: alk. paper)
  ISBN 978-1-60357-539-3 (ebook) (print)

  1. Fractions—Juvenile literature. 2. Arithmetic—Juvenile literature.
  3. Gardening—Juvenile literature. I. Title.

  QA117.B775 2012
  513.2'6—dc23
  2012034238

CONTENTS

Note to Caregivers:

Throughout this book, many questions are posed to the reader. Some are open-ended and ask what the reader thinks. Discuss these questions with your child and guide him or her in thinking through the possible answers and outcomes. There are also questions posed which have a specific answer. Encourage your child to read through the text to determine the correct answer. Most importantly, encourage answers grounded in reality while also allowing imaginations to soar. Information to help support you as you share the book with your child is provided in the back in the **Additional Notes** section.

Bold words are defined in the glossary in the back of the book.

An Idea Sprouts

This is the story of how our school, Sherlock Middle School, got a garden. We're in a small city surrounded by a lot of other cities. So, the sight of people gardening here might be unexpected.

The school has a huge, grassy field, and it is right next to a park. Some years ago, people living all around town got together with the teachers at the school to create a **community garden**. In a community garden, people share the garden space. Part of the garden was given to the school.

Later, the teachers and staff at Sherlock Middle School began to plan garden plots. And because the elementary school is a short walk away, they also invited teachers and students at Sherlock Elementary School to be involved.

The school gardens weren't always as green as they are now. To start the gardens, people had to dig up and clear out grass and weeds. The land was divided into plots, and space was left for future gardens and a tool shed.

Then, last year, some students began an after-school gardening club. The Garden Club was open to students from fourth through sixth grade. Some of the students worked with younger students, too, in their own garden plots. Even kindergarten students had space to grow plants. At the end of the school year, students in the Garden Club held a pizza party.

iMath *IDEAS:*

Operations with Fractions

Gardening often requires **operations** with **fractions**. That's because gardeners sometimes use parts of a whole, such as a part of a package of seeds or a part of a large bag of dirt. It's easier to add or subtract fractions if the fractions have the same **denominator**. So, gardeners rewrite fractions as **equivalent fractions**. Equivalent fractions have the same value.

You can **draw diagrams** to find equivalent fractions. Let's say that $\frac{2}{3}$ of one garden plot has been planted with beets. Beets have also been planted in $\frac{1}{4}$ of another plot that is the same size.

Each third can be subdivided into fourths. And each fourth can be subdivided into thirds.

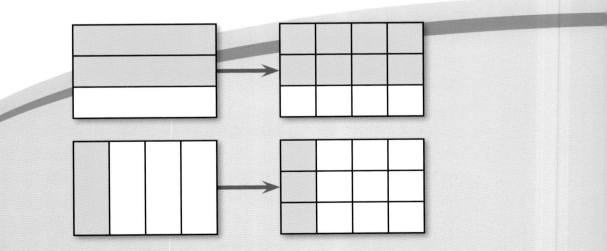

You can **add or subtract** equivalent fractions. What is the total amount of plot space that has beets?

You can **multiply** to rewrite fractions as equivalent fractions before adding or subtracting. To rewrite fractions as equivalent fractions, **multiply** the **numerator** and denominator of one fraction by the denominator of the other.

$$\frac{2}{3} + \frac{1}{4} = \frac{2 \times 4}{3 \times 4} + \frac{1 \times 3}{4 \times 3} = \frac{8}{12} + \frac{3}{12}$$

Now that the denominators are common, you can add the fractions easily.

$$\frac{8}{12} + \frac{3}{12} = \frac{11}{12}$$

$\frac{11}{12}$ of the garden are planted with beets.

You can add and subtract **mixed fractions**, too. Let's say that $1\frac{1}{4}$ rows are planted with Crazy Ruby beet seeds. $\frac{1}{2}$ of another row is planted with Rad Red beet seeds. All rows in this garden are the same length. How many more rows of Crazy Ruby beet seeds are there than Rad Red beet seeds?

To find this **difference**, first rewrite the **mixed fraction** as an **improper fraction**.

We can rewrite 1 as $\frac{4}{4}$. Then, add $\frac{4}{4}$ and $\frac{1}{4}$.

$$1\frac{1}{4} = \frac{4}{4} + \frac{1}{4} = \frac{5}{4}$$

Then, we rewrite $\frac{1}{2}$ as an equivalent fraction with a denominator of 4. $\frac{1}{2} \times \frac{2}{2} = \frac{2}{4}$. Now we can subtract: $\frac{5}{4}$ row $- \frac{2}{4}$ row $= \frac{3}{4}$ row

So, there is $\frac{3}{4}$ more of a row of Crazy Ruby beet seeds than Rad Red beet seeds.

Do you think adding and subtracting fractions can be helpful to gardeners?

You can also **Multiply and Divide Fractions**.

Multiply Fractions: Fifth-grade students plant flower seeds in $\frac{1}{4}$ of a plot. $\frac{3}{9}$ of those seeds are sunflower seeds. How much of the seeded plot contains sunflower seeds?

Set up a multiplication problem. Multiply the numerators. Then, multiply the denominators. The result you find is called the **product**.

$$\frac{3}{9} \times \frac{1}{4} = \frac{3 \times 1}{9 \times 4} = \frac{3}{36}$$

$\frac{3}{36}$ of the seeded plot are sunflower seeds.

Do you think multiplying fractions can be helpful to gardeners?

Divide Fractions: Some plants climb as they grow. A gardening shop sells 8-foot bamboo sticks. The students need sticks that are $2\frac{1}{2}$ feet long. How many $2\frac{1}{2}$-foot sticks can they get from one 8-foot stick?

First, write the math problem: $8 \div 2\frac{1}{2}$

Then, make a tape diagram to represent the 8-foot stick.

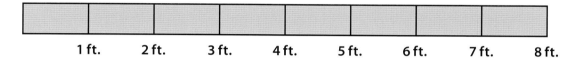

1 ft.   2 ft.   3 ft.   4 ft.   5 ft.   6 ft.   7 ft.   8 ft.

Use the diagram to find how many $2\frac{1}{2}$ foot sticks can be cut from this 8-foot stick.

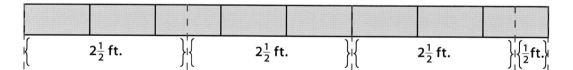

$2\frac{1}{2}$ ft. $2\frac{1}{2}$ ft. $2\frac{1}{2}$ ft. $\frac{1}{2}$ ft.

Dividing the 8-foot-long bamboo stick will give students 3 sticks, each $2\frac{1}{2}$ feet long. There will also be a small fraction of the original stick left over.

Do you think dividing fractions can be helpful to gardeners?

Materials
- pencil
- ruler
- string
- **tape measure in customary units of length**

Drawing a Map to Scale

Perhaps you will build a garden plot one day. Let's say that you are ready to begin planning now. How large will your garden be?

Find a place outside where you and your friends would like to have a garden. Lay down string to mark a rectangular space. This is an imaginary garden, so make it as large as you like.

Next, measure the rectangle's length and its width.

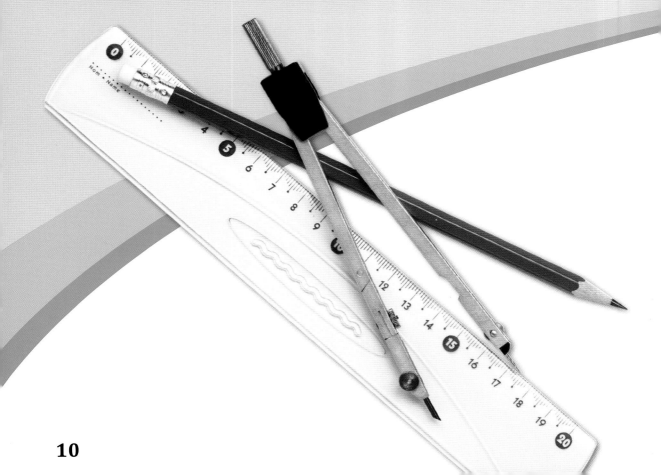

Now, make a scaled drawing of your garden plot. Let 1 inch on your drawing represent one foot of measure.

Draw the map scale on your paper. You can use regular paper, but using graph paper may make drawing easier. Use the map scale and a ruler to draw a scaled model of your garden.

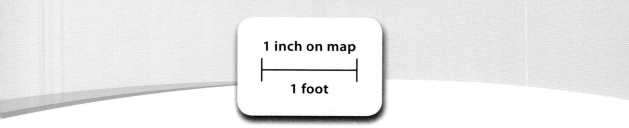

Now, imagine that you want to plant the following plants in your garden:

- eggplant
- broccoli
- cucumbers
- peppers
- tomatoes
- sunflowers

Divide the scaled drawing of your garden into as many equal sections as you like. Decide what you will plant in each section.

Label the sections with the names of the plants that will grow there. Think about how much sunlight your plants will need. Think about how wide or tall each plant will grow. Avoid crowding the plants.

Write fractions to represent how much of your garden each plant grows in.

Digging It!

The new gardeners had one thing to do before anyone could plant something new. They had to dig up the old grass and weeds before they could put in new garden plots.

While some students spent time digging up the school's garden area, other students were figuring out how to divide the space equally among the classes. That is, *if* they could divide it equally.

Sherlock Middle School had enough space for 10 community garden plots. The plan was for each plot to be a square that was 10 feet long on each side. The planned space also included space for pathways between the plots.

They assigned one plot per grade, from kindergarten through sixth grade. So, there were 10 plots to share with 7 classes.

A **ratio** compares two things and is often written as a fraction. For example, in this case, the ratio of the number of garden plots to the number of classes is ten to seven, or $\frac{10}{7}$.

Rewrite $\frac{10}{7}$ as a mixed fraction.

Eventually, the students decided that each class would definitely get one whole plot to work with. They did not decide how to use the remaining plots right away. But they needed to get digging! Spring was coming soon, and everyone wanted to be ready to plant seeds as soon as possible.

Students worked in groups of three to clear the garden space. In each group, two people used shovels to dig. This loosened the roots of the grass and weeds. Another person pulled the weeds and grass out of the loosened dirt and put them in a pile.

On the first day of digging, 30 students came out to work. Everyone worked at the same time. They used 2 shovels for each group of 3 students. So, the ratio of shovels used per group to the number of students per group was $\frac{2}{3}$. How many shovels did they use at one time? What is the best method for calculating the answer?

The Garden Grows

Many students brought in packs of seeds. They brought seeds for flowers, vegetables, and **herbs**.

Most of the students who brought vegetable seeds brought seeds for carrots, lettuce, and radishes. These plants grow well in colder weather, so the students could plant them early in the spring.

Students brought 36 packs of vegetable seeds. Of these packs, $\frac{1}{3}$ were carrot seeds, $\frac{1}{4}$ were lettuce seeds, and $\frac{1}{6}$ were radish seeds.

How many of the packs of seeds were for a vegetable other than carrots, lettuce, and radishes? What is the best method for calculating the answer?

What's the Word?

The scientific name for a radish is *Raphanus sativus*. The first part of that name, Raphanus, means "quickly appearing."

Radishes like the one in this photograph grow quickly in a garden, making them a favorite crop for beginning gardeners.

Companion Plants

Some plants keep bugs away. Peppermint, for example, keeps ants and **aphids** out of a garden. Aphids are tiny insects that suck juices out of plants.

The herb basil keeps flies and mosquitoes away. Rosemary is also an herb. It, like garlic, keeps away cabbage moths and carrot flies.

Companion plants are plants that grow well together because one plant keeps insects away from both of them. Marigolds and tomatoes are companion plants, for example. Marigolds keep aphids away.

A farmer donated four old wagon wheels to the Garden Club. Each wheel was divided into ten equal parts. Students lay the wheels on the ground and planted tomato plants, marigolds, basil, and rosemary in all of the sections inside three wheels. In the last wheel, students filled $\frac{2}{5}$ of the wheel with peppermint and $\frac{6}{10}$ with leeks. How many sections were filled with peppermint or leeks in all? What is the best method for calculating the answer?

The third-grade students grew lettuce seeds as an indoor project. They got 3 trays. Each tray had 100 parts.

Students planted a lettuce seed in each section. After about two weeks, they had hundreds of baby lettuce plants!

Baby lettuce plants sprouted in a total of $2\frac{1}{4}$ trays. How many baby lettuce plants sprouted? Remember, each tray has 100 parts.

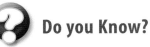 **Do you Know?**

Many people enjoy eating iceberg lettuce. But this isn't the plant's original name. The plant's first name was crisphead lettuce. That changed to iceberg lettuce when California farmers began shipping the plants under piles of crushed ice.

Each class was given some of the tiny lettuce plants to grow in their class plot. Fourth-grade students planted $1\frac{5}{8}$ rows with lettuce plants on one day and $2\frac{3}{4}$ rows on another day. How many rows of lettuce did they plant in all?

While the lettuce plants were growing in the garden, the students checked some gardening books to learn more about lettuce plants. They learned that lettuce belongs to the same plant family as sunflowers. They also learned that in the U.S., people eat about 35 pounds of lettuce per person each year.

The lettuce plants in this photograph are young. Some may need to be removed and planted somewhere else in the garden. This will give each plant room to grow.

Plants such as lettuce, carrots, and beets can grow when the weather is cool. Plants such as tomatoes, beans, and peppers prefer warmer weather. So, gardeners plant these a little later in spring. They wait until the chance of freezing weather is well past.

When it was time to plant beans, the students dug a small trench. Then, they placed the beans about 6 inches apart Bean seeds are easy to plant because they are actual beans! It is easy to see where to put them.

Students who planted bean seeds measured the plants' growth over time. One bean plant was $1\frac{1}{4}$ inch tall by the end of one week and twice as tall at the end of the second week. How tall was the plant at the end of the second week? Remember to write the answer in simplest form.

Mighty Earthworms

First-grade teachers helped their students build a Worm Box for the garden. The Worm Box is a plastic tub with a lid. It stays cool in a corner of the classroom. The box is half filled with soil, and the teacher brings in earthworms to live in the box. The students feed food scraps to the worms all year.

Earthworms are wonderful garden helpers. As they move through soil, they eat dead matter and bits of soil. They leave behind slime and material called **castings**. The worms' slime and castings are rich in material that helps plants grow.

Earthworms are amazing creatures. An earthworm is strong enough to move a rock that is 60 times its own weight. Earthworms are good eaters, too. One pound of earthworms, or about 1,000 worms, can eat $\frac{1}{2}$ pound of kitchen scraps per day. How many pounds of waste can a pound of earthworms eat in one full week?

Ladybird beetles help gardens, too. Most species of ladybird beetle eat aphids. A few types of ladybird beetles eat **fungi**, which can also harm plants. Some **midges**, which are tiny flies, also eat aphids.

The teacher for second grade bought a box of helpful garden insects from a garden supply company. The package had a mix of 250 midges and ladybird beetles. If $\frac{2}{5}$ of the insects were midges, how many ladybird beetles were in the box?

The students in the Garden Club created Garden Study Kits for everyone to use. Each kit contained a magnifying glass, a tape measure, and a glass jar with a rubber band and a piece of cloth.

When classes visited the garden, they brought kits and notebooks for writing notes and drawing pictures of plants and animals in the garden.

The Garden Club could not make enough Garden Study Kits for each student. So, they made kits for groups of five students. Each kit had 3 magnifying glasses. How many magnifying glasses did Garden Club members use to make kits for a class of 30 students?

Letting Things Rot

The Garden Club decided to use one plot for making **compost** instead of growing plants. Compost is recycled matter from once-living organisms. It can include food waste, such as **fruit**, vegetable, and meat scraps. It can include tree leaves, cut grass, paper, and coffee grounds. Tiny organisms in the soil break the waste down to make a soil rich in materials that help new plants grow.

A compost pile starts with a pile of dead plants. As the dead plants naturally rot, they give off heat. The heat helps break down material faster.

Some Garden Club students from sixth grade made compost bins. They used scrap pieces of wood boards. For one bin they used six boards that were each $2\frac{5}{8}$ feet long. How many feet of board did they use to make this bin?

For a second compost bin, the students used six boards that were each $2\frac{3}{4}$ feet long. How many feet of board did they use for this bin?

How many feet of board did the students use in all for both compost bins?

After the compost bins were built and the compost was started, families brought in kitchen scraps. The Garden Club students started more compost piles. In less than one year, they would have compost that the students could use in the garden plots!

Mixing, or turning over, a compost pile allows more air to enter. The oxygen in the air helps speed the breakdown of matter.

The members of this farming family are studying the yield of a corn plant. This will help them predict how much corn their entire crop will produce.

MATH AT WORK

When they plant a crop, farmers estimate the crop's **yield**. A yield is the amount of a product, such as corn, that a crop produces. This yield will determine how much a farmer can expect to earn for a crop, and how much he'll need to spend on planting future crops.

To estimate a corn crop's yield, a farmer measures areas of ground. Each section measures one foot wide and one foot long, or one square foot. Then, the farmer studies the plants that grow in that square foot. For example, if the farmer is studying an area of a corn crop, he studies the corn plants growing in that one square foot area. He counts the number of seeds growing on every corn plant growing in that square foot. Then, he multiplies that number of seeds by the total number of square feet the corn crop covers. The product gives the farmer a prediction of the crop's yield.

After **harvesting**, or collecting, their crops, farmers sell them. They keep careful records to know what they earn from selling their crops. They also calculate how much money they need to buy supplies like new seeds and equipment. For farmers, managing money is as important as caring for the crops.

Sunflower Heights

The fifth-grade class did a long-term project with one of the remaining plots. They planted some giant sunflowers along one side of the school garden. They used the measuring tapes in the Garden Study Kits. They measured heights of the sunflowers every two weeks.

The sunflower seeds were planted on the first day of spring, March 21. Ten days later, most of the sunflowers had sprouted. Two weeks after that, the students took the first measurements.

Gina, Darren, Alex, and Nora were a group. They each measured the height of a different sunflower and recorded their measurements in a chart like the one below.

Sunflower Height	
Gina	$18\frac{7}{8}$ inches
Darren	$19\frac{1}{8}$ inches
Alex	$18\frac{3}{4}$ inches
Nora	$20\frac{1}{2}$ inches

They wanted to find the **average** height of the sunflowers they measured. But to do that, they needed to find the sum of the four heights first. What was the sum of the heights of the four sunflower plants?

The giant flower we see on a sunflower is actually made of many tiny blooms that attract insects.

The next step in finding the average height was to divide the sum of the four heights by the total number of measurements. In this case, there were four measurements.

Divide the sum of the heights by 4. What was the average height of this group's sunflower plants?

Gina, Darren, Alex, and Nora measured heights of the same four sunflower plants until the end of school. After ten weeks, the average height of the sunflowers was $61\frac{5}{8}$ inches. That's more than five feet tall!

 Did You Know?

When a sunflower plant is young, it is heliotropic. The prefix *helio* means sun. The base word *tropic* means bend, curve, or turn. A young sunflower will turn to follow the sun, as the sun rises in the east and sets in the west each day.

Music from the Garden

With the remaining plot, the Garden Club grew gourds to prepare for a special music project they had planned for the following school year. Club members planted the seeds in the spring and let the plants grow over the summer.

The students estimated that $\frac{4}{5}$ of the gourd seeds they planted would grow into plants that produced gourds. They planted 31 gourd seeds. Of these seeds, about how many might they expect to grow gourds?

The Garden Club students' estimate was close. Their crop yielded 94 gourds. Later that year, in the autumn, the students planned to use the gourds to make colorful shakers for the school's music classroom.

Gourds come in interesting shapes, colors, and textures.

CONNECTING TO SCIENCE

In most places in North America, people plant seeds in the spring. The first official day of spring in North America is on or near March 21. This day marks the spring **equinox**. The word equinox means "equal night." At equinox, all parts of Earth have 12 hours of daylight and 12 hours of darkness.

After spring equinox, daylight lasts a little longer each day. This is a perfect time for planting seeds. Plants must have sunlight to grow. They also need warmth. Freezing temperatures kill the kinds of plants people grow for food.

The days grow longer. The greater amounts of sunlight warm the northern part of the planet. Then, we have summer **solstice**, what we call the longest day of the year. On this day, Earth's North Pole is tilted toward the sun. This means the South Pole is tilted *away* from the sun. Places on the southern half of the planet are experiencing winter.

Between summer solstice and the fall equinox in the Northern Hemisphere, there is less and less sunlight each day for North America. Plants make seeds. Crops ripen and become ready for harvesting.

Earth continues its orbit, and the seasons change again. The fall equinox is soon replaced by the winter solstice. Some plants lose their leaves. Seed plants die. The nights grow longer and colder.

Meanwhile, on the southern half of the planet, the days get longer and warmer. Spring comes, and people plant seeds for gardens and crops. Eventually, spring turns to summer and plants continue to grow.

Each year, the third-grade students study native plants. Most years, they use part of their plot in the garden to plant wildflowers. The Garden Club's teacher gets seeds from a gardening store. The seeds are sold by the pound.

The students mark off a section of their garden plot. Then, they scatter the seeds. The students take notes on when flowers appear on the different plants. They describe the flowers and try to identify them. They watch to see what insects are in the garden.

This year, the second-grade students wanted to grow some wildflowers, too. The third-grade students had $\frac{1}{4}$ pound of seeds. They gave the second-grade class $\frac{1}{8}$ pound of the seeds. What fraction of a pound of seeds did the third-graders have left?

Most classes at Sherlock Elementary do a Bug Counting project in late spring. First, students get into groups of four or five. They pick up a Garden Study Kit from the members of the Garden Club. Then, they choose a plot to explore in the community garden.

Each group member looks at one part of the plot. They record the number and kinds of insects they see in their area.

This year, Jenna found spiders, ladybird beetles, ants, and other beetles. Of the insects she saw, $\frac{2}{3}$ were ants. She counted a total of 27 insects. How many ants did Jenna count?

Near the end of each school year, it's time to let the worms out of the Worm Box. After months of eating food scraps, the worms have created wonderful compost.

Worms do more than make soil richer. As they wiggle through soil, they make space for water and air to move through the soil. This helps plants, whose roots take in air and water.

The first-grade students have taken care of the earthworms all year. They estimate that there are about 2,000 worms in the box by the end of the year. The students usually scoop $\frac{1}{4}$ of the worms and soil from the box into their garden plot. They give the rest to the Garden Club plot.

How many worms are added to the first-grade plot?

It's a Fruit

And of course, by the time summer gets near, the harvesting begins! This year, students have grown carrots, turnips, beets, and potatoes. These are all called **root vegetables** because the root of the plant is the main part people use for food.

People eat the leaves of plants such as lettuce and spinach. These are sometimes called leaf vegetables. The green leaves of beet plants are also very tasty to most people. Many people use spinach and beet leaves in salads. Others cook the leaves before eating them.

Some things people call vegetables are actually fruit. For example, any kind of squash is a fruit. This includes pumpkins! Tomatoes are also fruit. Anything with seeds inside is a fruit of the plant it grew on.

The Chickens Are Coming!

A few years after the community garden was started, community members joined together to start a chicken coop. Residents from the neighborhood signed up to help take care of the chickens. Then, each week they got some of the eggs the chickens laid.

This year, they want to put new chicken wire around the fence that surrounds the coop. Chicken wire is a wire mesh. The openings are in the shape of a hexagon. The chickens are safe inside the coop area, and they get plenty of air and light.

There are usually a few Garden Club students who are interested in learning more about the chickens. This year, they helped build the coop. They measured the length of each side.

The fence was planned as a rectangle, but the corners aren't quite square. The shorter sides measure 10 feet and $9\frac{11}{12}$ feet. The longer sides measure $20\frac{3}{4}$ feet and $19\frac{5}{6}$ feet. How long of a roll of chicken wire did the students use in all?

The students also helped build new ramps for the chicken coop. Adults cut the long, flat boards for the ramps and smaller pieces of wood to put across the ramps. Chickens use these like rungs on a ladder. The smaller pieces give them something to step on as they go up and down a ramp.

To make a set of rungs, an adult began with a slender piece of wood $84\frac{1}{2}$ inches long. She cut it into pieces $11\frac{1}{2}$ inches long. How many whole short pieces did she get from each longer piece?

Did you know that chickens like to eat watermelon? You can cut a huge watermelon into a few pieces, and scatter the pieces on the ground. The chickens stand on and around the pieces, pecking at the fruit.

You can give chickens special feed. But chickens naturally eat grass, many kinds of bugs, and some of the plants people consider weeds. Some of the weeds and grass students pulled in the garden are fed to the chickens in the community garden.

Plants don't grow well if they're overcrowded. The roots have to compete for space, water, and air. So, students pulled some of the plants that were growing to make room for other plants.

There were 40 lettuce plants in a small space. Some students pulled $\frac{3}{4}$ of the plants and fed them to the chickens. About how many small lettuce plants did the students feed to the chickens?

Getting Ready for Summer

Gardeners use a variety of tools in their work.

Summer, of course, is the season that begins just as the school year ends. The Garden Club always has projects to get ready for the fall, the season when school starts again.

All the fruits, roots, and flowers that are ready must be harvested. Otherwise, they will rot on the plants. Other plants die and need to be put in the compost. And then there are the compost piles to care for.

? What's the Word?

The word *season* has different meanings. For example, different sports are played at different times of the year. These times are called seasons. We also use the word *seasons* to describe spring, summer, fall, and winter. But the word *season* originally referred to growing food. It comes from a Middle English word meaning "to plant seeds."

Every summer, some students volunteer to work in the garden. They pull weeds that grow and feed some to the chickens. They harvest vegetables, fruit, and some flowers.

They take care of the compost piles, too, by checking them, turning them over, and spraying a little water on them.

Garden volunteers keep some of the crops they harvest for themselves. The school donates the rest of its flowers, vegetables, and fruit to local **charities** that help feed people in need.

One summer, volunteers picked $25\frac{1}{2}$ pounds of tomatoes. The tomatoes were divided among three charities. How many pounds of tomatoes were given to each charity?

When students signed up to be summer volunteers, members of the Garden Club gave them lists of things to do. They also provided a schedule of when adult volunteers would be there to help.

Student volunteers spend about $\frac{1}{4}$ of their time caring for plants. This includes harvesting and cutting off dead flowers. They spend about $\frac{1}{2}$ of their time weeding. The other $\frac{1}{4}$ of their time is spent doing a variety of chores, such as turning compost or cleaning tools.

In his first week as a volunteer, Jaxon worked $12\frac{1}{2}$ hours. How many hours did he spend weeding?

Pizza Party Planning

Green peppers growing

Before school ends and summer vacation begins, the Garden Club has a pizza party. This year, they planned to use vegetables from plants in their garden as pizza toppings. These included tomatoes, green peppers, onions, and garlic.

Members found a recipe for pizza sauce that volunteers could make at home. The main ingredient was $1\frac{3}{4}$ pounds of ripe tomatoes.

How many pounds of tomatoes did they need to make twice the amount of sauce the recipe makes?

How many pounds of tomatoes did they need to make three times the recipe?

They also planned for everyone in the club to get at least 2 pieces of pizza.

At the party, each pizza was cut into 8 equal slices. So, each person got $\frac{2}{8}$ of a pizza. There were 23 members in the Garden Club this year, including the teacher who helped them. How many pizzas did they make for the party?

Finally, the school year was over, and summer volunteers were hard at work. They have gardening plans for the summer and new ideas for next year. Then, like a gardener, the Garden Club can start all over again.

Late in the summer, but before the new school year began, someone donated wood to the Sherlock Community Garden. The wood was thick and strong, an excellent material for making raised garden beds. Raised garden beds lift plants from the ground, making it easier for people to take care of the plants.

Student and adult volunteers worked together to make one bed. They used two short pieces at each end and two long pieces for each length.

Each short piece was $2\frac{1}{3}$ feet long. Each long piece was $4\frac{2}{5}$ feet long. How many total feet of boards did they use to make the bed?

How can they calculate the answer?

They want to find the amount of feet needed for the short sides first. So, they could add or multiply the fractions.

Add Fractions. Add fractions together to find the sum.

$2\frac{1}{3} + 2\frac{1}{3} + 2\frac{1}{3} + 2\frac{1}{3} =$ amount of feet needed for the short sides

$4\frac{2}{5} + 4\frac{2}{5} + 4\frac{2}{5} + 4\frac{2}{5} =$ amount of feet needed for the long sides

Then, add the sums to find how many feet are needed to build all four sides.

Multiply Fractions. Multiply the fractions to find the product.

$2\frac{1}{3} \times 4 =$ amount of feet needed for the short sides

$4\frac{2}{5} \times 4 =$ amount of feet needed for the long sides

Then, add the products to find how many feet are needed to build all four sides.

Will you add or multiply to solve this problem?

Gardeners decorated the raised beds in this community garden.

Did you find the amount of the short sides to be $9\frac{1}{3}$ feet and the amount of the long sides to be $17\frac{3}{5}$ feet?

Or, did you change the amounts into improper fractions and find the amount on the short sides to be $\frac{28}{3}$ feet and the amount of the long sides to be $\frac{88}{5}$ feet?

Either way you still have to find the total number of feet used to make the bed. You may want to use equivalent fractions to find a common denominator before adding.

$9\frac{1}{3}$ feet $+ 17\frac{3}{5}$ feet $=$ total number of feet

or

$\frac{28}{3}$ feet $+ \frac{88}{5}$ feet $=$ total number of feet

What is the total length of all the pieces of wood used to make one garden bed?

The bed will make gardening even easier, especially for some of the youngest and smallest gardeners!

WHAT COMES NEXT?

A new way to build chicken coops is becoming very popular. The new model is called a "chicken tractor." The *chicken* part of the name is obvious. It's a place for chickens. The *tractor* part means that the chickens' home can be moved around.

When chickens are moved around to different parts of a yard, they eat grass, weeds, and bugs in many places. This keeps the yard and the chickens healthy.

A chicken tractor has two parts. One is a coop. The other is a fenced-in area. The coop and fence are connected so that they can move as one piece. Being movable also means that the chicken tractor must be made of sturdy materials.

Visit a library or go online to learn more about chicken tractors.

- List the materials that work best for building chicken tractors.

- Explain how the coop and fence are connected.

- Using what you learn, design a chicken tractor. It must be movable and safe for the chickens. Draw a diagram of your chicken tractor.

- Add special features to the chicken tractor to make it clear that it is your original design.

Share your design with someone who raises chickens or with members of a community garden. Perhaps someone will help you build your chicken tractor. Then, you may be able to get some chickens of your own.

GLOSSARY

aphids: small bugs that suck so much liquid from plants that they kill the plants.

average: one number that describes all of the other numbers in a set.

castings: the waste products of earthworms.

charity(ies): an organization that cares for people in need.

community garden: a shared public space in which individual people or groups each garden a plot of land.

companion plants: plants that grow well together because one of them keeps insect pests away from the other.

compost: what's left after once-living things rot, or decay. Compost includes grass, leaves, and food waste.

denominator: the number of equal parts into which a whole is divided, shown as the number below the line in a fraction.

difference: the result of subtracting one number from another.

equinox: the point in Earth's orbit when the sun is over the equator and the length of day and night is equal for the whole planet.

equivalent fraction: a fraction that has the same value as another fraction, but has a different numerator and denominator.

fraction: a quantity that stands for a part of a whole.

fruit: a sweet, fleshy product made by a tree or plant, that carries seeds on the inside.

fungi: a kingdom of living things that includes molds, rust, and mushrooms.

harvest (harvesting, harvested): the gathering in or collection of a crop.

herbs: plants used in spices and medicine.

improper fraction: a fraction with a numerator larger than its denominator. An improper fraction can be rewritten as a mixed fraction.

midges: tiny flies.

mixed fraction: a quantity that includes a whole number and a fraction.

numerator: the number of equal parts described by a fraction, shown as the number above the line in a fraction.

operations: actions such as addition, subtraction, multiplication, and division of numbers.

product: the result of multiplying two numbers.

ratio: a comparison of two numbers of measures using division.

root vegetables: vegetables whose roots are a source of food.

solstice: the two times of the year when the sun reaches its highest or lowest point in the sky, and the northern and southern halves of Earth experience the shortest or longest day.

yield: the amount of product that a crop produces in one growing season.

FURTHER READING

FICTION
Seedfolks, by Paul Fleischman, HarperTrophy, 2004
NONFICTION
Storey's Guide to Raising Chickens, by Gail Damerow, Storey Publishing, 2010
Dig, Plant and Grow, by Louise Spilsbury, Heinemann Library, 2010

ADDITIONAL NOTES

The page references below provide answers to questions asked throughout the book. Questions whose answers will vary are not addressed.

Page 12: $1\frac{3}{7}$

Page 13: 20 shovels

Page 14: 9 seed packs were for a vegetable other than carrots, lettuce, and radishes.

Page 15: $\frac{10}{10}$, or 1 whole wheel

Page 16: 225 lettuces

Page 17: $1\frac{5}{8} + 2\frac{3}{4} = 1\frac{5}{8} + 2\frac{6}{8} = 3\frac{11}{8} = 4\frac{3}{8}$ rows

Page 18: $1\frac{1}{4} \times 2 = \frac{5}{4} \times 2 = \frac{10}{4} = 2\frac{2}{4} = 2\frac{1}{2}$ inches

Page 19: $7 \times \frac{1}{2} = \frac{7}{2} = 3\frac{1}{2}$ pounds

Page 20: 100 were midges and 150 were ladybug beetles.

Page 21: $\frac{3}{5} \times 30 = \frac{18}{1} = 18$ magnifying glasses

Page 22: $15\frac{6}{8}$ or $15\frac{3}{4}$ feet

Page 23: $16\frac{2}{4}$ or $16\frac{1}{2}$ feet for this bin; $32\frac{1}{4}$ feet for both

Page 25: $77\frac{1}{4}$ inches

Page 26: $19\frac{5}{16}$ inches

Page 27: $24\frac{4}{5}$ seeds, or about 25 seeds

Page 30: $\frac{1}{8}$ pound of seeds left

Page 31: 18 ants

Page 32: 500 worms

Page 35: $60\frac{1}{2}$ feet; 7 whole wooden pieces

Page 36: 30 plants

Page 38: $25\frac{1}{2} \div 3 = 25\frac{1}{2} \times \frac{1}{3} = 5\frac{1}{6} = 8\frac{1}{2}$ pounds

Page 39: $6\frac{1}{4}$ hours

Page 40: $3\frac{1}{2}$ pounds; $5\frac{1}{4}$ pounds

Page 41: 6 pizzas

Page 44: $26\frac{14}{15}$ feet, or $\frac{404}{15}$ feet

INDEX

CONTENT CONSULTANT

David T. Hughes

David is an experienced mathematics teacher, writer, presenter, and adviser. He serves as a consultant for the Partnership for Assessment of Readiness for College and Careers. David has also worked as the Senior Program Coordinator for the Charles A. Dana Center at The University of Texas at Austin and was an editor and contributor for the *Mathematics Standards in the Classroom* series.